Participatory Curriculum Development in Agricultural Extension Education

NIPA® GENX ELECTRONIC RESOURCES & SOLUTIONS P. LTD.
New Delhi-110 034

About the Author

Dr. M. Shivamurthy is an Emeritus Scientist-ICAR, Department of Agricultural Extension, University of Agricultural Sciences, GKVK, Bengaluru. He is also serving as Member, Board of Management, University of Horticultural Sciences, Bagalkot. Prior to this he was a Professor (HAG) and Head of the Department. He has 35 years of experience in teaching, research and extension activities and has guided eight Ph.D and twenty four M.Sc research scholars. He has also served as Fellow of Indian Society of Extension Education and Visiting Professor (Ghent University, Belgium and Humboldt University, Berlin). As PI and Co-PI of several national and international research projects funded by ICAR, Coconut Development Board, Department of Biotechnology GOI, DIS & Wageningen Agricultural University, The Netherlands and Japanese Bank of International Cooperation; he has visited many countries viz., France, South Korea, Germany, Iran, Belgium, Isreal, United Kingdom, Australia and Egypt as part of research activities. He has organized many training programs, winter and summer schools. He is an active member of editorial and executive committees for professional societies and has published more than hundred research articles in national and international journals and thirteen books. His contribution in the field of extension was honored with several awards like Dr.O.P. Dhama Memorial Award, ISEE National Fellow Award, Dr. G.S. Vidyarthi Memorial Natioanl Award, Best paper presentation award and state level award for best agricultural book publication.

Dr. A. Madhushree is working as Research Associate in Emeritus Scientist Project, Department of Agricultural Extension, University of Agricultural Sciences, GKVK, Bengaluru. Prior to this she has worked as Senior Research Fellow in Integrated Farming System Demonstration Project and Zero Budget Natural Farming Project. She also served as Assistant Professor on contractual basis in the Department of Agricultural Extension, UAS, GKVK, Bengaluru. She was a recipient of Rajiv Gandhi National Fellowship and has cleared ASRB-NET and UGC-NET. She has attended international conference at Singapore and conferred with Young Scientist award. She is a recipient of Best thesis and Best oral presentation award. She has developed folders and training modules, authored and co-authored several research papers, review papers, book chapters for national and international journals.

Participatory Curriculum Development in Agricultural Extension Education

M. Shivamurthy
Emeritus Scientist ICAR
Department of Agricultural Extension
University of Agricultural Sciences, GKVK
Bengaluru, Karnataka

A. Madhushree
Research Associate
Emeritus Scientist Project
Department of Agricultural Extension
University of Agricultural Sciences, GKVK
Bengaluru, Karnataka

NIPA® GENX ELECTRONIC RESOURCES & SOLUTIONS P. LTD.
New Delhi-110 034

NIPA® GENX ELECTRONIC RESOURCES & SOLUTIONS P. LTD.

101,103, Vikas Surya Plaza, CU Block
L.S.C.Market, Pitam Pura, New Delhi-110 034
Ph : +91 11 27341616, 27341717, 27341718
E-mail: newindiapublishingagency@gmail.com
www: www.nipabooks.com

For customer assistance, please contact
Phone: + 91-11-27 34 17 17
Fax: + 91-11-27 34 16 16
E-Mail: feedbacks@nipabooks.com

ISBN: 978-93-58875-52-2

Composed and Designed by NIPA.

Preface

Development of Toolkit for Participatory Curriculum Development majorly builds on experiences of participation and is becoming recognized more widely as a critical element in the success of agricultural education. In the process of participatory curriculum development. we followed participatory approaches like Focus Group Discussions and Field level Workshops involving extension teachers, UG & PG students, field extension workers and farmers. The main steps of the PCD approach adopted here have high practical utility for the design of formal course contents for the Undergraduate and Postgraduate courses in Agricultural Extension. A great deal of thinking is required while deciding on how much participation will be required from which type of stakeholders, at what level(s). While developing this toolkit we emphasized more on practical utility and articulation of 'participatory curriculum development' and relating to the redesigning of course contents and making it more relevant in the present context of present-day challenges of farming community. We have also discussed why teaching and learning should be participatory and what benefits we get by adopting participatory approaches. It is hoped that it will be an inspiration for all those who embark on a curriculum reform exercises with the objective of improving the quality and efficiency of agricultural education. We hope the toolkit developed in this project will serve as a stepping-stone for adoption of participatory methods while developing the curriculum for new subjects in agricultural extension and reorienting the existing curriculum to accomplish the present-day job market by producing quality manpower to address present day challenges.

Authors

Contents

1

Introduction

Participatory curriculum development (PCD) in extension education is an emerging approach to help and improve the quality of education in farm universities. The main steps of the PCD approach adopted here have high practical utility for the design of formal course contents for the Undergraduate and Postgraduate courses in Agricultural Extension. A great deal of thinking is required while deciding on how much participation will be required from which stakeholders, at what level(s). Here we have considered, what do we mean by 'participatory curriculum development' and how does this relate to developing the course contents and designing a course? We have also discussed why teaching and learning should be participatory and what benefits we get by adopting participatory approach. We have discussed who can participate in curriculum development and to what extent. Based on our experiences we have also listed here what participatory curriculum development actually encompasses and the main phases one should follow while put it into practice.

Development of Toolkit for participatory curriculum design majorly builds on experiences of participation and is becoming recognized more widely as a critical element in the success of agricultural education. Fact of the matter is that, in spite of concerted efforts over the years on improving agricultural extension education at the farm universities, the general comments is that, teaching is not effective and not developing the graduates to meet the present day job market at the field level to bring pragmatic changes among the farming community. Many traditional approaches to curriculum development and the resulting curriculum have not brought the outcome as it was expected. One of the major reason we attribute for this may be that, curriculum development rarely involves the different groups or individuals who will gain from, or have something to offer. It is widely accepted that, curriculum development is more likely to bring about effective results if participatory approach is used. Besides, considering the absence of a well-designed toolkit in the country we have attempted to develop toolkit by involving different stakeholders in the field of Extension education.

Reorienting existing agricultural extension education to address sustainable development is very much needed and necessary, so that all the stakeholders like agricultural students both UG and PGs, teachers in extension education, field extension workers and farmers, can gain knowledge, skills, perspectives and values of sustainability so as to assume responsibility for creating a sustainable future lifestyle. However, the crucial point is to have teachers who can deliver the reoriented lessons and teach students on emerging knowledge and skills leading to become best extension workers by meeting the agricultural production, productivity and marketing aspects of the farmers.

The reorientation of the curriculum in extension education have taken various forms with an expectation from students to become mastery of content and must possess specific skills and capabilities such as problem solving or decision making, with this the students must feel comfortable in a variety of contexts to demonstrate that they have mastered the learning, which should be relevant and transferable to other contexts. As a consequence, curricula are likely to be much more flexible and responsive to individual needs, offering significant local autonomy within a framework of common principles and content standards. The emphasis is on a balance between assessment of teaching and assessment for learning. We can look back in history and find out that the word curriculum originally came from a Latin word, which meant a running race, lap around the track, course. Curriculum development describes all the ways in which a training or teaching organization plans and guides learning. It can take place in an institutional setting like a school, college or training centre, or in a village or a field. It is central to the teaching and learning process and includes all the planning and guiding of learning by a training or teaching, whether it is carried on in groups or individually, inside or outside a classroom, in an institutional setting or in a village or field (Rogers and Taylor, 1998).

Curriculum development is conceptualized as the development of strategies that guide the processes that ensure knowledge deemed necessary is taught and learned. It is a concept that implies going beyond the traditional notion of curricula as mere syllabuses of prescribed content. Indeed, it is commonly suggested that in order to effectively foster learning, educational content, methods (diversity of pedagogical strategies to support learning processes) and structures (time, physical space, human resources and leadership) need to be permanently adjusted according to evolutions in science, technology, culture, economy and social discourse.

Operationally we define curriculum development as ways in which agricultural educational institutes formally plans and guides teachers and students at the farm university colleges and it is central to the teaching and learning process.

This description implies that, curriculum development take place in many settings and involve many people. Typically, agricultural extension curriculum development involves two main issues:

1. Identifying what learning is needed and type of teaching to be provided to meet the learning needs
2. Planning, delivering and evaluate the teaching so as to make it more effective

These issues can be addressed in different ways but it is important that the approach we use here have led to effective teaching. In this context, this toolkit strongly recommends participatory approach to agricultural extension curriculum development since this will bring the best results and lead to real-time useful learning.

Why sound curriculum development is important?

Curriculum development provides an opportunity for institutionalizing a systemic approach to learning. It aims at integrating the recognition of the needs for learning, the ways in which learning is organized and delivered and the way in which learning is monitored and evaluated within a particular context of location, values and beliefs. If curriculum development is carried out efficiently and effectively, the learning needs of learners will be met, teachers will teach more effectively, using suitable, relevant methods and materials, a good service will be delivered, satisfying the demands of different stakeholders, and the goals and aims of the education and training objectives will be achieved.

There is a growing perception that curriculum development so far has not led to effective extension education and training as the following quotes suggest:

- Over the years, the production, processing, marketing, consumers demand for the quality food and living standards of farmers and consumers have changed tremendously which led to higher expectations from the extension to address the related challenges of the farmers. Agricultural education and training have failed to adapt and respond to the realities of rural societies. Contrary to this, over the years' agricultural extension curricula and teaching methods and tools often have been developed that are not relevant to the development objectives to meet the needs of farmers (FAO, 1997)
- Reorientation of agricultural extension curriculum is essential to the formation of a new extension education system, as the curriculum is the basic and primary element of agricultural educational change. At the same

time, this area can be the most difficult to change, since many teachers and extensionists are comfortable with the existing system and they resist changes in curriculum, teaching and learning practice (Shao, 2000).

Participatory processes have been identified as one of the most powerful engines to provoke real transformations in agricultural universities and non-government organizations and ICAR institutions, in order to help them, and those with whom they engage, face the growing demands and challenges(Taylor, 2003). In this context, those who are interested in giving the PCD approach a try should be aware that many critical issues remain and demand careful consideration. This attempt does not constitute a blueprint or a list of strict recommendations for PCD. Instead, it provides some basic guidelines and aims at helping those interested in adopting the PCD process by asking the right questions rather than try to come up with all the right answers.

2

Purpose of this Toolkit

- To explain the main concepts and elements of a participatory curriculum development process
- To present practical skills and knowledge leading to the effective design of teaching and learning
- To build confidence of the learners in applying new methods and approaches to teaching and field extension work.
- To demonstrate application of participatory approach in development of Extension curriculum

This Toolkit emphasizes an active learning approach, based on the process of experience, reflection and action. The key principle is that people do not learn simply by passive listening. They need to be involved from beginning of the training and designing of the program. This approach challenges traditional roles of teachers and students (class room situation) or trainers and trainees (field situation). To use this Toolkit effectively, teachers and trainers need to reflect on their own roles in the learning process. They are in need to become learners, along with other participants in training program besides, they need to understand and practice effective facilitation and communication skills, as well as improving their technical knowledge. The new paradigm in curriculum restructuring is to generate curriculum ideas from a broad spectrum of society, and to achieve national consensus on curriculum goals as part of the curriculum reform process.

The Toolkit has been written for a diverse audience

- Agricultural training teams who might want to redesign training program and use this toolkit as a reference,
- Resource persons involved in the planning, organizing and implementation of a training courses
- Trainers and educators teaching agricultural related subjects at national or regional institutions,

- Subject matter specialists who have been in capacity building programs at the state and national level contributing one or several subjects of a training event and
- Workers in pre-service and in-service training institutions and Personnel involved in or interested in promoting participation,

3

Concepts of Curriculum Development

"Curriculum" is seen often as a critical issue during discussions on quality of agricultural education, being considered variously as content, as product and as process. It is easy to make the assumption that a common understanding of curriculum, but in practice this is far from the case, with a host of definitions, approaches and ideological standpoints. Even though a dialogue on curriculum theory is well established, there is still a strong tendency in practice to understand curriculum as a list of content, often developed in considerable detail, that students should be taught. In trying to deal with the complexities of curriculum, Rogers and Taylor (1998) suggested that curriculum development describes ways in which a training or teaching organization plans and guides learning. Important qualities of curriculum development are:

- Curriculum development is a flexible, dynamic process leading to products such as new or revised curriculum frameworks or detailed curricula which include objectives or learning outcomes, content and means of assessment and evaluation of learning. It can also involve identification and use of appropriate teaching and learning methods and materials - it is not a list of content.
- Curriculum development is about planning and guiding - it is not a blueprint or a recipe.
- Curriculum development can include anyone and occur anywhere – it is not exclusive.

4

When to Reorient the Curriculum

Curriculum reorientation is necessary, when any one in use is no longer responsive to the needs, interests and unable to meet the demands of the farming community to which it is intended to serve. In any case a number of factors, such as those listed below, must be taken into consideration while reorientation:

- There should be an analytical assessment of the existing agricultural extension curriculum in order to justify any proposed reorientation.
- Learning needs of the farm university graduates and farmers should be reviewed from the point of view of both individual learner requirements and national development needs.
- A consensus relating to curriculum reorientation must be established.
- Agricultural extension curriculum objectives, content and methods must be appropriately determined.
- Evaluation and feedback procedures must be established and used.

Though it is a lengthy and laborious process to satisfy all the above criteria. However, the extent to which curriculum reform brings about the desired change will depend on the attention given to the above points.

5

Issues Leading to Curriculum Restructuring

As stated before, a careful assessment of the existing curriculum is essential before any modification is undertaken and must take into account the country's education policy, political, economic, demographic, cultural, social and technological environment. Problems of farmers to be solved, needs to be satisfied, and priorities to be identified and addressed and then only the recommendations made for action. Major changes in the objectives of extension education, content and methods of extension teaching used in the curriculum should be reviewed, against the background of existing agricultural educational achievement and the constraints that have to overcome.

6

Approaches to Curriculum Development

- **Content approach**

We can identify several different 'traditional' approaches to curriculum development. The most common approach until recently is the 'content' approach. This is where the curriculum is basically a list of knowledge – things that the agricultural graduating learners need to know. Usually this list is made by a curriculum development committee or group of experts identified at the national level. The content approach usually results in a curriculum, which is very theoretical, academic, and based on the extension discipline. In this approach, the teachers receive little or no guidance on how to facilitate the learning process.

- **Product approach**

Another approach commonly used is the 'product' approach. In this case, the focus is on what the agricultural students will be able to do (and the knowledge and skills they require) after the course has finished. This approach usually follows a systematic planning procedure, and assumes that there are common goals for the learners, with the provision of adequate expertise, resources and technology. Setting agricultural extension objectives is an important part of this approach.

- **Process approach**

The 'process' approach is characterized by the recognition of individual perception and behavior. It adopts a less structured procedure, and is based upon an appreciation that understanding and knowledge on a process of constantly shifting interactions. The 'content' and 'product' approaches are more closed, uniform, predictable and safe. The process approach results in a more open, varied and unpredictable curriculum.

Which approach to use?

We cannot say that one of these approaches is always better than the others, although the content approach is least likely to result in successful learning and is not recommended. Both the product and process approaches have definite advantages and disadvantages. The analysis of the situation at the national level helps to decide which approach is most suitable. For example, where a job and the tasks are very clearly defined, then a product approach should be very effective, as long as individual learners' requirements are taken into consideration. Where it is difficult to identify specific job-related competences, it may be better to have a more open-ended process approach, whereby the teachers can constantly review the learning needs as they progress through the learning process.

Whether a product or a process approach is used, it is vitally important to identify who is involved in curriculum development, and ensure that all the groups and individuals who have a real interest or stake in the course are able to contribute to the curriculum development or curriculum reorientation process. This often does not happen; the product approach is usually carried out in a very top-down way. Manpower planning, is an example of a product approach and is often done at a very high level of government where few people make decisions on behalf of many others.

7

Importance of Participatory Curriculum Development

Real benefits are obtained when we use a participatory approach to curriculum development and reorientation. Primarily, the course contents we provide and the learning will become more effective. If students participate actively in the learning process, then they are more likely to learn and teaching is more likely to be effective. They will have more ownership in the teaching, because their needs will have been identified and hopefully they will also be involved in deciding how their needs can be met. This will increase their motivation, which will help them to learn more effectively.

Benefits of participatory curriculum development or reorientation:

- Greater opportunities for discussion and reflection with different stakeholders (people and groups who have an interest in the teaching). This will help everyone learn, and work together more effectively.
- Forming links and networks will become easy, which will allow teachers to share information better than before; courses will become more relevant to the local context.
- Some groups of students and individuals who do not normally have a 'voice', such as girl students, students from rural and poor background may become included in the discussions and they will benefit more as a result.
- Possible to establish a dynamic course design process as new linkages and lines of communication resulting in greater satisfaction with the course and offering the course.
- Different stakeholders can gain greater responsibility for various stages of the curriculum development and reorientation process; this increases the motivation and commitment of everyone who participates.

With this we can summarize that, through participatory curriculum development and reorientation approach agricultural extension courses will be become more effective and the benefits will be more sustainable.

8

Weakness Noticed in the Existing Methodology of Recommending Changes in Curriculum

In the present system of curriculum changes, participation of all the stakeholders are not actively involved in developing curriculum over the years. This led to develop the course contents unable to develop extension workers to articulate the present day problems of farmers and offer solutions to present day complex problems of farmers.

Curriculum development is more likely to be effective if it is undertaken by applying participatory approach in true sense. Hence, there is a need to adopt participatory methodology involving all the stakeholders in curriculum development. This is an emerging approach to improve the quality of education and training. Involving stakeholders in a meaningful way, drawing upon their experience and insights in to curriculum planning, implementation and evaluation builds on our experience helps in achieving success of extension education and training.

8

Weakness Noticed in the Existing Methodology of Recommending Changes in Curriculum

[illegible]

[illegible]

9

Procedure Followed in the Study for Development of PCD Toolkit

While developing the toolkit for Participatory Curriculum Development participatory approaches like Focus Group Discussions and Field Level Workshops were adopted. The goal is to provide demand-driven services and to do so, extension professionals need to respond for farmers' requests rather than deliver predetermined packaged solutions. It is also time to enable the farmers to empower and make their voices heard. Equally important is to make the service providers accountable to the farmers, which is possible when the farmers pay for the services they receive. The challenges include offering new services, ensuring the quality of services, and strengthening collaboration and synergy among extension service providers. Extension professionals with current knowledge who are able to make informed decisions about agricultural systems and who have skills needed for adaptation and facilitation can make significant contributions to extension services and thus to agricultural development. Hence, to know the effectiveness of extension services at the field level, focus group discussions and field level workshops were conducted with different stakeholders. In the present study stakeholders considered are; Undergraduate, PG and PhD students, Extension Education Teachers, Field Extension Workers and Farmers.

Focus group discussions were conducted with field extension workers, Extension professionals in the State Agricultural Universities (SAUs), Para extension workers, Farmers, Undergraduate &Post graduate and Ph.D Scholars as below.

Details of FGDs conducted

S. No.	Participants	No. of Programs	No. of participants	Date of conduct
1	Field Extension Workers	3	28	25.02.2022
2	M.Sc. Students	2	29	10.03.2022
3	Ph.D Scholars	2	28	29.03.2022

4	Para Extension workers	3	115 (3 batch)	09.07.2022 11.07.2022 12.08.2022
5	ADA/AO/AAO	2	25	21.09.2022
6	Extension Professionals (Teachers)	2	18	11.10.2022
7	UG Students	3	60	17.10.2022
8	Farmers	3	56	18.10.2022

Photographs of FGDs conducted

Focus Group Discussion (FGD) with Field Extension Workers regarding important skills and competencies

Focus Group Discussion (FGD) with PG Students

Focus Group Discussion (FGD) with Para Extension Workers

Data collection from PG Students and Focus Group Discusion (FGD) with Farmers

Focus Group Discussion and field level workshop

Workshop for Field Level Extension Workers

10

Field Level Workshop on Capacity Needs Assessment and Development (CAN &D)

The motive behind conducting the workshop on Capacity Need Assessment and Development is that the existing Extension Advisory Services (EAS) needs new capacities to respond effectively to the emerging challenges in agricultural development. Undertaking Capacity Needs Assessment and Development is critical for organizing appropriate Capacity Development (CD) interventions. Lack of a clearly articulated list of core competencies for EAS adversely affects the recruitment of new staff, professional development of existing staff, as well as the quality of professional education in extension. Hence, field workshops were organized on the theme of capacity needs assessment and development which is an effective mechanism for gathering different perspectives across different actors. Several stakeholders representing the public and private sector are involved in EAS provision represented in the workshop. Interactions for the key agencies involved in the CD of EAS would help in understanding the methods used to assess training needs and other CD gaps, approaches used for capacity development, their strengths and limitations.

11

Group Discussions Conducted to Know the Opinion on Revised ICAR 2021 BSMA Syllabus of Extension Education

To address the present day problems in agriculture and horticultural sectors and also to equip the graduating and postgraduate agricultural students, the ICAR has been continuously striving to bring necessary reforms for quality enhancement in agricultural education. The Council has appointed National Core Group and BSMA Committee for revision and restructuring of Post-graduate and Doctoral syllabi in consultation with all the stakeholders to meet the challenges and harness opportunities in various disciplines of agriculture and allied sciences. It has been felt that a paradigm shift is necessary in academic regulations to comply with various provisions of National Education Policy-2020. The syllabus of Masters' and Doctoral programs was restructured and new courses were introduced.

Core objectives of developing this tool kit is to apply participatory methods for reorienting curriculum of agricultural extension to prepare the students of farm universities to confidently address the emerging challenges in agricultural transformation and development. With this background, participatory methods were adopted to elicit the opinion of different stakeholders regarding the effectiveness of extension services, critical job skills and competencies required by extension workers and the coverage of skills and competencies in the existing curriculum. Keeping these points in view observations and opinions were recorded through participatory methods. New skills and competencies were identified which are very important for effective performance of job by extension workers. Hence, it was felt necessary to take the opinion of stakeholders regarding the recently revised syllabus of Extension Education as per ICAR 2021 Broad Subject Matter Area (BSMA) Committees. An attempt has been made to know the importance of course contents recommended in the revised syllabus. To achieve this, data were collected from teachers and Post Graduate students of Department of Agricultural Extension, University of Agricultural Sciences, GKVK, Bengaluru and University of Agricultural and Horticultural Sciences, Shivamogga using 3-point continuum scale (Most important, Important, Notimportant) to understand the importance of course contents in each course.

Courses recommended by ICAR 2021 BSMA Committee

M.Sc courses	Ph.D courses
Major courses • Extension Landscape, EXT501 (2+0) • Applied Behaviour change, EXT502 (2+1) • Organizational Behaviour and development, EXT503 (2+1) • Research Methodology in Extension, EXT504 (2+1) • Capacity development, EXT505 (2+1) • ICTs for agricultural extension and advisory services, EXT506 (2+1) • Evaluation and impact assessment, EXT507 (2+1)	**Major courses** • Policy engagement and extension EXT 601 (2+1) • Methodologies for social and behavioural research EXT 602 (2+1) • Technology commercialization and incubation EXT 603 (2+1) • Educational technology and instructional design EXT 604 (2+1)
Minor courses • Managing Extension organizations, EXT508 (2+1) • Enabling Innovation, EXT509 (1+1) • Gender mainstreaming, EXT510 (2+1)	**Minor courses** • Risk management and climate change adaptation EXT605 (2+1) • Livelihood development AEE 606 (1+1) • Facilitation for people centric development EXT607 (2+1)

Group Discussion with research scholars of Department of Agricultural Extension, UAS, GKVK, Bengaluru

Stakeholders involved in participatory curriculum reorientation:

- Students UG
- Students PG and Ph.D.
- Extension Education Teachers
- Field Extension workers
- Farmers (combination of BF, SF, and MF)

12

Results Obtained from Participatory Approaches (Focus Group Discussions and Field Level Workshop)

The results of Focus Group Discussions and Field Level Workshops (Tables presented at the end of toolkit) conducted with different stakeholders mentioned in the methodology revealed that, communication skills, soft skills, leadership development skills, personal and professional development skills followed by entrepreneurship development skills are more important and needed to perform job effectively at field level extension work (Table 1). The result indicates that there is a need to revise the existing curricula where the updated content and it needs to be taught at the UG & PG level so that the needed capacities to work at the field level can be acquired.

Appropriate ways to acquire the required competencies and skills

- Reoriented or updated curricula including more of practical and applicability skills
- Need to provide internship opportunities at different stages during Bachelor's degree
- Provision of training and capacity development workshops at working environment.
- Strengthening and Improvement of core competencies among field-level extension officers.

The opinion of stakeholders (PG students and teachers) regarding the revised syllabus of Extension Education of ICAR 2021 Broad Subject Matter Area (BSMA) Committee presented in Table 2 and 3 revealed that, capacity development, ICTs for agricultural extension and advisory services followed by managing extension organizations are important courses for post graduate students.

Table 1 : Importance of job skills and core competencies required by agricultural extension workers for effective performance

Sl. No.	Skills	Field Extension Workers (n=28)	Para Extension workers (n=115)	ADA/AO/ AAO (n=25)	M.Sc Students (n=29)	Ph.D Students (n=28)	UG Students (n=60)	Farmers (n=56)	Teachers (n=18)
1	Program Planning skills	0.84	0.83	0.86	0.85	0.85	0.87	0.92	0.81
2	Program implementation skills	0.84	0.82	0.88	0.91	0.88	0.88	0.91	0.89
3	Enhancing efficiency& effectiveness of Extension	0.82	0.82	0.80	0.88	0.86	0.88	0.90	0.83
4	Communication skills	0.91	0.88	0.85	0.94	0.93	0.95	0.95	0.92
5	ICT Skills	0.86	0.84	0.87	0.90	0.88	0.90	0.93	0.95
6	Program Evaluation skills	0.85	0.86	0.77	0.86	0.83	0.87	0.89	0.85
7	Professional development skills	0.89	0.85	0.81	0.96	0.91	0.98	0.87	0.89
8	Personal skills	0.89	0.81	0.82	0.90	0.85	0.90	0.88	0.90
9	Technical expertise and marketing skills	0.88	0.83	0.83	0.89	0.93	0.92	0.94	0.85
10	Leadership and Management skills	0.86	0.85	0.84	0.94	0.90	0.95	0.91	0.88
11	Entrepreneurship development skills	0.82	0.84	0.83	0.93	0.91	0.88	0.89	0.92
12	Soft skills	0.90	0.87	0.86	0.97	0.92	0.77	0.91	0.96

Table 2 : Ranking of important M.Sc. courses as expressed by stakeholders on revised ICAR 2021 BSMA syllabus of Extension Education

Sl. No.	Courses	Mean Index Scores	Ranking
1	Capacity development	0.99	I
2	ICTs for agricultural extension and advisory services	0.92	II
3	Managing Extension organizations	0.90	III
4	Enabling Innovation	0.90	III
5	Gender mainstreaming	0.89	V
6	Research Methodology in Extension	0.89	V
7	Evaluation and impact assessment	0.88	VII
8	Extension Landscape	0.88	VII
9	Applied Behavior change	0.87	IX
10	Organizational Behavior and development	0.87	IX

Table 3 : Ranking of important Ph.D. courses as expressed by stakeholders on revised ICAR 2021 BSMA syllabus of Extension Education

Sl. No.	Courses	Mean Index Scores	Ranking
1	Methodologies for social and behavioral research	0.91	I
2	Risk management and climate change adaptation	0.91	I
3	Policy engagement and extension	0.89	III
4	Technology commercialization and incubation	0.88	IV
5	Livelihood development	0.88	IV
6	Facilitation for people centric development	0.88	VI
7	Educational technology and instructional design	0.84	VII

With respect to Ph.D courses, methodologies for social and behavioural research, risk management and climate change adaptation, Policy engagement and extension followed by technology commercialization and incubation are the important for doctoral students.

Based on the results of participatory methods adopted in the study, it is proposed that, identified skills and core competencies which are very important can be included particularly at the Undergraduate level and the importance of proposed skills were also identified by taking the opinion from all the stakeholders is shown in Table 4.Majority have expressed soft skills and technical skills are most important for extension worker to perform better at field level followed by specialized skills and process/functional skills. Ultimately, this has tremendous implications for preservice training curricula (undergraduate levels) in agricultural extension education (Scheer *et al.*, 2006). With this background a set of core skills recommended were listed as follows:

1. **Soft Skills:** Soft skills are character traits and interpersonal skills that characterize a person's relationships with other people. Soft skills include the personal attributes, personality traits, and communication abilities needed for success of extension workers on the job.
2. **Process/Functional Skills:** Skills which enable extension workers to interact with others to perform tasks which are having practical utility. Skills used to manage and modify actions using appropriate tools to complete a task or organizing a task into logical sequence for successful completion.
3. **Specialized Skills:** These are the skills leads extension workers to become experts in a particular field. Specialized means extension worker is trained or developed for a particular purpose or area of knowledge.
4. **Technical Skills: These** are the job-specific knowledge and techniques needed to proficiently perform tasks that require particular expertise. Technical skills typically require the use of certain tools and technologies required to use those tools.

Table 4 : Importance of proposed core competencies and skills

Sl. No.	Skills/competencies	Mean Index scores	Ranking
1	Soft skills	0.95	I
2	Technical skills	0.86	II
3	Process/ Functional skills	0.85	III
4	Specialized skills	0.85	III

The rationale behind considering these broad skills is that undergraduate level is the important phase where graduates need proficiency to perform certain tasks and get expertise by attaining the abilities to perform the job effectively. It is found effective to train graduating students with these skills which intern help them to get expertise. The individual skill/ competency or any activity considered as skill can be grouped among these proposed core competencies depending upon the situation and purpose. We have grouped some individual skills and competencies among each is as follows.

1	Soft skills	• Analytical and comprehensive skills • Good relationships and rapport with people • Time management strategies
2	Process/ Functional skills	• Facilitate access to credit • Inputs and output services • Networking and partnership building • Acquire and Allocate Resources (Resource Mobilization) • Conduct participant observations • Establish a Model Village • Development potential and agro ecosystem analysis
3	Specialized skills	• Collaborate to implement extension programs • Agribusiness promotion • Risk identification • measuring, analysis and evaluation • Facilitation skills • Design services based on gender analysis
4	Technical skills	• Rural livelihood and social welfare • Working out end to end solutions • Climate change and sustainability • Value chain and trade • Reaching and involving members of marginalized groups • Develop a Grant Proposal • Outline a stakeholder participation strategy • Assess stakeholder influence and importance

Based on the results obtained from the participatory methods adopted in the study, the important core skills and competencies essential in the present day to job market to bridge the mismatch between manpower demand and availability were listed out and recommended in the report to include in the UG curriculum. Recommended core skills and competencies exposure at the undergraduate level helps the graduating students to perform their job effectively at the field level extension activities. With this background, a toolkit is developed by adopting participatory methods in the process of curriculum development.

13

Methodology Recommended for Participatory Curriculum Reorientation

1. Participatory curriculum reorientation awareness-raising workshop for key stakeholders: In the present study focus group discussion and workshops were conducted to know the effectiveness of present curriculum of extension education with different stakeholders (Students UG, PG and Ph.D, Extension teachers, Field extension workers and farmers). Data were collected by using schedules regarding the important contents of present curriculum and most important for extension workers in the present situation to be included in curriculum
2. Follow-up workshops with group of stakeholders were conducted: The opinion and responses given by stakeholders were recorded, analyzed and important contents were identified as expressed by them. Also, the opinion on revised curricula recommended by ICAR BSMA syllabus were recorded and analyzed.
3. Need assessment: Core skills and competencies required for effective functioning at field level were identified.
4. Reorienting/development of curriculum frameworks (blueprint) within agricultural extension curriculum: Preparation of blueprint where inclusion of the identified core skills and competencies in the curriculum wherever it is necessary in the extension courses.
5. Reorienting detailed curricula
6. Learner-centered teaching methods (TOT)
7. Learning materials development training
8. Testing of new/revised curricula
9. Monitoring of new/revised curricula
10. Institutionalization of the curriculum

14

Steps Recommended to Conduct Participatory Curriculum Development

Identify main reasons and purpose of curriculum development and key areas needed by stakeholders for curriculum change. This can be done by adopting participatory methods like Focus group discussion/ field level workshops. Carry out stakeholder analysis and identify specific potential areas suggested by stakeholders to be included in the curriculum for better performance at the field level and their likely role in the process. In order to encourage greater stakeholder involvement invite stakeholders such as staff and students from various farm universities, field extension workers and farmers. The procedure adopted in the study using participatory methods to identify key areas are mentioned in the methodology recommended for participatory curriculum reorientation to follow where conduct of group discussions and workshops and follow up of participatory methods has to be done to identify and analyze the requirements of stakeholders.

I. Follow-up of participatory methods adopted and need assessment

Inorder to validate the results obtained from participatory methods adopted to identify potential areas from stakeholders. Introduce concept of PCD process and discuss potential for application at the institution level. Identify organizational issues which need to be addressed for curriculum change to go ahead. Validate and revise main steps for action.

II. Needs assessment

Plan and carry out Contents Need Assessment (CNA) as suggested by stakeholders. Then prepare the outline of modifications/changes need to be made in the existing courses by identifying range of Knowledge, Skills and Attitudes (KSA) required by field level extension workers, consolidate results, obtain feedback on results from fellow professionals. The main purpose of needs assessment surveys is to identify the strong and weak elements in existing courses and to find ways of improving the quality of the learning they provide. Needs assessment exercise identifies what the stakeholders expect the curriculum to achieve and describes what it actually accomplishes.

III. Development of curriculum frameworks

Review the existing curriculum based on results of CAN, aims of curriculum, main learning objectives, main topics and main content areas. Provide overview of the methods to be used and resources required. Gather and review existing learning materials. In this context two approaches can be used: (1) development of curricula by individual university faculties, involving local stakeholders and (2) development of curricula by collaborative groups of teachers from different universities. Both approaches have been very valuable grounds for learning. Collaborative groups of teachers from different universities could provide an opportunity to feed stakeholder views and inputs gathered by each working institution through curriculum need assessment, FGD, workshops and other events into the overall curriculum development process. With participation of teachers from different universities, curriculum frameworks can be developed for subjects, including contents, justification, objectives, and topic order.

IV. Develop detailed curricula/modify existing curriculum based on curriculum frameworks

Write detailed content, time, teaching methods, teaching materials, etc. Specific plans should be worked out to provide for practice and a practical training course for each subject or for the whole course. Emphasis should be given to move from a "teaching" approach to a "learning" approach. Since education of students training requires acquiring skills and attitudes as well as knowledge. Teachers should be encouraged to move beyond a merely theoretical approach. Preparation of learning objectives is key to this. Hence the important points to be considered while developing detailed curricula or modification of existing curricula are:

1. Identifying Critical Areas for Reform-It is important to identify for each area of the curriculum to be reformed.
2. Introduction and Institutionalization of the modified Curriculum-A detailed plan should be prepared for the introduction and institutionalization of the reformed curriculum.
3. Identify Available Resources- Within resource limitations the most urgently needed aspects of the reform should be undertaken. The curriculum reform process could be phased according to the resources available, starting with the most critical areas.

4. Strategy for Curriculum Monitoring, Evaluation and Improvements- The framework should include a strategy for supporting and making the curriculum adaptable to the needs of the various learning groups.
5. Determine by subject area, the essential competencies to be achieved by all students, the content required for enrichment and those items to be retained from existing curricula.
6. Outline the various teaching approaches and ensure that they are consistent with the curriculum.
7. Outline the curriculum assessment and evaluation strategy, identifying what would improve curriculum assessment and feedback.

V. Develop Learner-centered teaching methods and training

Develop capacity of teachers or trainers to plan and apply new, learner-centered teaching and training methods. Teachers or trainers should be trained well on the use of learner-centered teaching methodologies such as group work, FGDs, facilitation skills, making presentations, and making use of case studies and role plays. A participatory approach should be adopted in development of teaching and learning materials. Training should be provided on concepts of the use and development of learning materials, followed by more hands-on training in learning materials production. As a result, examples of innovative learning materials produced includes teaching notes, case studies, project outlines, guidebooks and manuals, all of which will have to be used in combination with alternative strategies for teaching and learning.

VI. Testing of modified curricula

Implement modified curricula with groups of students/ trainees, evaluate and adapt curricula as required. Developed learning materials or modified curricula should be tested by obtaining feedback from experts or subject matter specialists in the concerned subject from all universities, also feedback should be obtained from students and other stakeholders who were invited to comment. This can be considered as first step of evaluation process.

VII. Monitoring of curriculum reform is essential

It is the process by which the results of an evaluation are used to improve the modified curriculum implementation process. Monitoring requires a systematic collection and organization of data and information related to the elements included in a curriculum. Such information may reveal which of the stated objectives of the curriculum are given greater emphasis than others, which instructional materials are available and in which magnitude, number of teachers available to teach and how many are needed. The purpose of the exercise is to ensure that remedial action to be taken quickly.

VIII. Institutionalization of the curriculum

This is the process of incorporation of reformed curriculum into academic programs. This process is carried or decided to take care of planning and implementation of curriculum to bring necessary reforms for quality assurance in education. There may be committees for revision and restructuring of syllabi in consultation with all the stakeholders to meet the challenges and harness opportunities in various disciplines of agriculture and allied sciences. Respective committees has to take due care by following flexible, multi-disciplinary and holistic approach while developing the syllabus regulations. Through intensive discussion with the subject experts and based on the feedback from the faculty and students, the syllabus can be restructured and new courses may be introduced.

15

Capacity Development for Curriculum Implementation

The concept of capacity development is defined in various ways. Broadly, it is defined as a process by which skills, and knowledge are built, utilized, retained and nurtured with a view to provide an entity responding to a development challenge. Two components that are vital in any plausible definition of the concept are human skills (the ability to perform a task) and institutions (effectiveness and efficiency of organizations, systems, processes and procedures). Knowledge is a distinct component of the definition, because it allows for the combination of skills, experiences, insights, expert intuition and actionable recommendations from research, to enable an entity to continuously innovate and apply best-practice solutions to emerging and evolving challenges. The application of knowledge makes skills and institutions dynamic and responsive.

In this situation, capacity development is understood as the process of assisting an individual or a group to gain the insight, knowledge and experiences required to solve problems and implement change.

Conclusion

Agricultural education plays a pivotal role in driving sustainable development by enhancing the intellectual and technical growth of students graduating in agricultural sciences. However, the effectiveness of this role hinges upon the practicality of the content and syllabus covered by teachers in each subject. The transformation of current agricultural education, both at the undergraduate (UG) and postgraduate (PG) levels, is imperative to equip students with the ability to tackle real-world challenges in the field and meet the technical requirements of farmers.

Participatory Curriculum Development involves a process of involving endusers in the creation of curricula. It is founded on an understanding of the knowledge, skills, attitudes, and beliefs necessary for individuals to perform specific tasks. The objective of the presented Participatory Curriculum

Development process is to formulate curricula and tools that support a range of diverse learning programs.

The toolkit has been crafted to uphold this fundamental approach, aiming to facilitate hands-on learning and contribute to wider processes of societal transformation. It acknowledges the existence of various methods for restructuring and developing curricula. The Participatory Curriculum Development process outlined in this toolkit is based on the findings of the current study, along with insights drawn from research on curriculum reform in developing countries. It is envisioned that this toolkit will serve as an inspiration for those embarking on curriculum reform endeavors, aiming to enhance the quality and efficiency of agricultural education.

We are confident that the toolkit developed will act as a cornerstone for the incorporation of participatory methodologies in the development of new subjects in agricultural extension. Furthermore, it seeks to guide the reconfiguration of existing curricula to align with the demands of today's job market, thereby producing competent professionals capable of addressing contemporary challenges.

References

Chambers, R. (2002). Participatory workshops: a sourcebook of 21 sets of ideas & activities, Earthscan, Londres.

Vui, Dang Kim, Thuan, Dinh Duc, Cai, Hoang Huu and Taylor, P. A Case Study of Participatory Forestry Curriculum Development and Revision in Vietnam, Rome: FAO. (in press).

FAO. (1997). Issues and opportunities for agricultural education and training in the 1990s and beyond. Rome: FAO.

FAO. (1993). Trainer's Guide: Concepts, principles and methods of training, with special reference to agricultural development. Vol. 1. Rome: FAO.

Goldstein, I. L. (1993). Training in organizations: Needs assessment, development, and evaluation. Thomson Brooks / Cole Publishing Co.

Helvetas. (2002). 10 key stages towards effective participatory curriculum development - learning from practice and experience in the Social Forestry Support Program, Vietnam, and other Helvetas-supported projects. Experience and Learning in International Cooperation no. 2. Zurich: Helvetas

Kolb DA. Experiential learning: Experience as the source of learning and development. Prentice-Hall, Englewood Cliffs, NJ 1984.

Lynton, R. P., & Pareek, U. (2011). Training for development. SAGE publishing India.

Rogers, A., & Taylor, P. (1998). Participatory curriculum development in agricultural education. A training guide.

Rogers, A. (1999). Participatory Curriculum Development: A Case Study in Agricultural Extension. In Convergence, Vol. XXVI, No. 2, 1993.

Rowntree, D. (1981). Educational Technology in Curriculum Development.London: Harper and Row, xviii + 296 pp.

Shao Xiarong, and Bruening, T.H. (2000), Curriculum Development Changes in Chinese Agricultural Schools. Paper submitted to the 17th Annual Conference of the Association for International Agricultural and Extension Education.

Taylor, P. (2003). How to design a training course- A guide to participatory curriculum development. London: VSO/Continuum Vietnam, April 16-19, 2000.

Taylor, P. (2000a). New perspectives, new curricular. A case study of participatory curriculum development in forestry education in Vietnam (paper presented at the workshop on changing learning and education in forestry Sa Pa.

Taylor, P. (1998). Participatory curriculum development for agricultural education and training: experiences from Viet Nam and South Africa.

Index